VAN DER STEEN'S *Cats*

Van der Steen's
CATS

WITH AN ESSAY BY

D.J.R. Bruckner

·

Van der Steen About Himself

translated by Ralph Read

Fromm International Publishing Corporation

NEW YORK

Library of Congress in Publication Data

Steen, Germain Van der, 1897-1965.
Van der Steen's cats.
Translation of: Van der Steens unheimliche Katzen.
1. Steen, Germain, Van der, 1897-1965.
2. Cats in art.   I. Title.

N6853.S79A4 1984 759.4 84-18777

ISBN 0-88064-018-9
Printed and bound in West Germany

VAN DER STEEN'S *Cats*

WHAT is going on here? Cats, just cats, among things they like, being shown off. They are extraordinarily modest, for, despite the peculiarities of his style and vision, Van der Steen leaves one's imagination alone with the cats and not only with his cats, but with cats. Whole galleries of artists, and writers and musicians, have tried to bring metaphors out of the idea of cat. There is no success in this pursuit. Van der Steen seems to have abandoned metaphor and gone after the cats.

Pablo Neruda in a little poem suggested that not the moon's light or the shadows it throws, nor even flowers, could suggest the palette of one's notion of a cat. "He is good to think on, if a man would express himself neatly," Christopher Smart wrote of his cat, Jeoffrey. It is no easy thing to do. Here is Eleanor Clark on one colony of cats among the many in Rome, this one inhabiting ruins at one end of the Piazza Vittorio Emmanuele: "They are also of the most extraordinary colors. It is a botanical garden of exotic furs, in every combination; marmalades shading to bronze, orange in trout specklings on grey or black, a single contrasting or striped forearm on a monotone coat, every kind of bib and dashing including the common chest triangle, often only one perky ear of solid color like an insistent strain of nobility through the conglomerate birth; but they are all aristocrats though of a dead-end breed, even the ones with back sides and front sides of two utterly incompatible schemes, blue-grey and white in front and black with orange behind, like a blue-faced mandrill or a polychrome bust from the late Empire; or say a pansy bed took to sprouting mammals, some plain white with only the golden circles of the eyes or all black as pansies can be, which now stalk or rest among the other furless flowers that they would never permit themselves to break any more than if they were of rare porcelain on a mantelpiece."

Every cat loves flowers, or almost any plant, tree or vine. Until one gets used to it, it is startling to see cats looking out at one from under leaves of a bush, the limbs of a tree, tall grass on a lawn. Van der Steen thought often about flowers—less successfully than about cats, but often impressively. In his watercolors of flowers the shapes of stem and blossom are odd, the leaves of the stems as brightly colored as the blossoms which sometimes hang in midair with no support. But if one steps back and looks at them, they are unquestionably flowers as they are in the mind and in the eye. Van der Steen's cats like flowers the way cats like flowers.

Perhaps a vision is the only adequate sight of cats. Unless one descends to the language of scientific classification which obliter-

ates differences, a common description seems impossible. Abyssinians, Manx, Angoras, Siamese, Persians of many hues, Somalis, Chartreux, Himalayans, Japanese bobtails, Egyptian Maus (silly name; the Egyptians call them simply cat [*mau*], a word which obviously springs from the cat's mouth), calicos, cameos, chinchillas, tortoiseshell, an infinity of mixed breeds and markings, with eyes amber, orange, blue, black, emerald, violet, sometimes of two different colors.

"Its face is broad like a Lyon," the early naturalist William Salmon said. But the heads can be almost any shape, and even the broad faces may look oval, round, triangular, square, and in profile protuberant, flat, semispherical. And there are almost as many kinds of conscious tails as cats—wands, ferns, fans, stumps, ostrich feathers, straight, curled, kinked. Even one cat has many more different aspects as it changes position than other animals have; a tabby Persian rearing up on its hind legs may seem to have ten paws poking out from the great shield of billowing fur shimmering from shin to tail. Pity the painter; even the wild spawn of languages is not enough to cover cats. "Tabby" is merely the Arabic *attabi*, which refers to a watered silk with its undulating lines. It is the domesticating of cats that has undone our imagination; for a cat of virtually any marking or color, let loose again into the wild, will produce within a few generations offspring that are tabby.

Germain Van der Steen had a vision of cats—and of other

animals, notably birds. His birds don't quite make it; they always look as though they are warding off his imagination, shying away from his camera. But his imagination entered into cats and they into it, and his cats might be part of nature. His cats' paws are good. We imagine we always see them, nails and all, but we seldom do, because the cat keeps the business end of its paws out of sight most of the time. And his cats' whiskers he may have seen not from our point of view but from the cats'. They are fine, but more than the stuff of vanity, for as any child knows, a cat with clipped whiskers will misjudge its proximity to objects and stumble into things. The magnitude of the whiskers on Van der Steen's cats is proper. And the eyes of his cats are natural, radically different from those of countless nineteenth-century pictures of cats all with olive-shaped eyes and pupils like slits. Everyone knows that most cats see better in shade or dusk than in full daylight and that they have a third lid to protect their eyes, but it is rare to see a cat looking at you with pupils folded into parentheses; if you watch them obsessively, you will catch them looking that way, but not often. The eyes of Van der Steen's cats are open—round, square, intent, reflective, some of them reflecting or *chatoyant*, as his Paris neighbors would have said in the old days; in his vocabulary this *chatoyancy* is a manifest joke.

But he was making something more than jokes. In the few years before his death two decades ago, there was a certain amount of critical appraisal and journalism about Van der Steen in Eu-

rope, especially in France where he was born. The few who took his pictures very seriously may have misjudged them even more than those who dismissed them as whimsical. He was praised by a few powerful artists, treasured by a group of collectors, patronized at some good exhibitions. A search of the catalogue of words used about him is not inspiring—"simple," "wondering," "primitive" (he was commonly called *un naif* in France), "undistracted." He was said to owe much to expressionism, or to Gauguin and Rousseau among others, or to van Gogh since he came from a Dutch family. One can see Gauguin's colors in Van der Steen's work; but hardly Gauguin's cats, not the cat in his enormous allegorical canvas and certainly not the one in the foreground of his portrait of Pierre Loti, which almost is photographic except that Gauguin made the stripes appear to have been painted on the cat. Van der Steen may have learned something from van Gogh, especially his deep gaze. He sometimes conveys a notion of the ticking of cats' hair, the wandering of color from dark to light or the other way around in each hair from root to tip, much in the way van Gogh gives the many shades of a blade of sun-struck grass.

But perhaps this is to take criticism too seriously. Who knows whether the critics had ever bothered to look at cats? An artist can find plenty of cats on canvas to imitate or learn from, especially in nineteenth-century French works. One need only think about Ambroise Vollard, the great art publisher who was passionate about cats. Virtually all of the painters he promoted painted portraits of him in his gallery with one or another of his cats. Manet illustrated a book about cats by Champfleury, and there is even a cat in his startling *Déjeuner sur l'Herbe*. Hundreds of cats in paintings of the era, as though they sprang unbidden right out of the brushes. And behind them stand at least four hundred years of cats in paintings and drawings. Dürer's engraving of the Fall of Man has a cat in the foreground; Leonardo da Vinci drew a Madonna and Child with cat; Tintoretto has a cat attending the Last Supper; there are many cats in Brueghel and Bosch. In England Gainsborough, Hogarth and Joshua Reynolds all depicted cats, and in Spain practically every artist did—Goya's cats are famous and those in Velázquez's *Tapestry Weavers* are wonderful testimony to the distinct quality of Spanish cats.

The search for the ancestors of Van der Steen's cats, which have little in common with the literal renderings of all these predecessors, might be more successful among some ancient objects—the splendid glass tumblers imperial Roman artists decorated with leopards in magenta or blue; the temple, ceremonial and mythic cats in many cultures, from Egypt to Thailand to the Temple of the Cat in Tokyo, from stone cats on medieval cathedrals to the great cats distorted and compressed in the facades of Aztec and Mayan monuments or woven in blazing colors into the borders of some of their tapestries.

Van der Steen

The small critical lexicon about Van der Steen's cats used by the journalists and critics included "fantastic," "startling," "visionary," "unnatural," in German *unheimliches*—which may be fantastic but also has an undertone of the eerie or bewitched that betrays the anthropomorphism which was creeping in, into the vocabulary, not into the cats. Gustave Doré's famous illustrations for Charles Perrault's "Puss in Boots," the gallant cat as musketeer, is anthropomorphic; Marc Chagall's cat in the painting of *Paris Through the Window* has a human profile; the cats of Kalighat that were so popular at the turn of the century, with their Persian eyes complete with indigoed lids, were anthropomorphic; so was Beatrix Potter's Simkin. Van der Steen's cats may stretch one's understanding of feline, but they are not in that other tradition.

It has also been said that one or another of them is thespian, rabbinical, episcopal, imperial, vampish; someone even found a Zoroastrian magus in one. Well, cats may play roles among themselves, but we are not privy to the mimicry. The words are ours, the acts and inspirations theirs, and it is a nice question whether the human roles imitate the animals' or theirs ours. Montaigne cannot have been the first to wonder whether he was not more sport to his cat than she was to him. I suspect a cat, introduced to a gallery of Van der Steen's pictures of cats, might be disconcerted and made uncomfortable by the suspicion that someone who was not a cat had realized a good deal of what cats

are up to. That is the sense in which they are amusing. That thought gives little comfort to an ailurophile, of course, for the question is always whether the cats like us.

One can live with a cat for many years and never be sure of the answer. Its possession of a house, alley, yard or garden, and of all other living things in those places, is an assumption of authority made as naturally by a small cat as the domination of forest, veld, mountain or jungle is made by its great lordly relatives. Cats are kings not simply because, as the poet Richard Eberhart put it, they "survive by force"; it is their lineage that elevates them. They come from a family whose precedence is nearly absolute, and who can be sure cats are unaware of that? The very word "cat" recedes into antiquity beyond the grasp of philologists who cannot find its origins. It turned up in Latin and Greek—*cattus*, *kattos*—two millennia ago even though those languages had other words to designate the animal; it is known from the earliest records of every European language used from Ireland to Siberia in a very narrow range of variations—*gato*, *kater*, *kattuz*, *kot'ka*, *kotchka*, *katti*—on "cat," a word that is recognizable also in very old Middle Eastern, Indian and North African languages.

But only old in terms of millennia, which are nothing to cats. The antiquity of cats is known, but it cannot be imagined easily. From fossils we know that animals easily recognizable as the ancestors of modern cats lived forty million years ago, at a time when other mammals were of such strange configurations that they can be related to later inhabitants of the animal kingdom only by difficult and often uncertain conjecture. The great cats, much as we know them, walked on the earth from Europe to China and Africa, and from Alaska to Tierra del Fuego, ten million years ago; they were ancient when the first little ancestors of mankind were struggling to walk upright.

The small cats were not far behind the great ones. The basic pattern of cat was quite successful from the beginning, and to a cat we might be the progeny of big infants who started late and stumbled slowly through evolution. The close resemblance of all cats of all sizes everywhere is more marked than that of members of any other animal family. And if there are glimpses of tiger, serval, lynx or caracal in Van der Steen's cats, they are also in cats one meets along the road or in the yard, some with eyes like those of Peter Porter's "King of the Cats," which

> *burned low and red so that drunks*
> *saw them like two stars above a hedge.*

Blake's burning tiger looks out from the forest eyes of a cat sitting in the window of a city apartment straining and squinting to mark the movements of pigeons or people across the street.

A cat's self-absorption, so often explored by poets who want to talk more about poets than about cats, is not some feline secret, although it is related to the secret of cats' survival. The cat is simply presocial. It never ran in packs and it survives alone better

Vander Steen

than any other animal. "Domesticated" is the wrong word for a cat, no matter how long it and its forebears may have lived in homes. There are many cases on record in which a house cat has been turned loose in the wild and has become very large and aggressive, some becoming up to forty inches long and weighing thirty-five pounds, very like the European wildcats from which the familiar house cats descended. The cat's prodigious adaptability is intimately related to its solitude. It possesses the sovereign power of loneliness, but also the gift of friendship; a cat does not keep itself apart much except when it is ill.

Old Tiney, the hare that was the pet of William Cowper two hundred years ago, slept in the same box with Cowper's cat, the poet tells us in the rabbit's epitaph. Everyone knows Mark Twain's account of a cat he met one hundred years ago in the zoo at Marseilles that had taken up with an elephant, playing around his hooves without worry and then climbing up his legs to sit on his back in the sun for her nap. It is not uncommon to find cats living in barns and stables with cows, horses, goats, owls and dogs. They even live around chickens without attacking them, chasing after sparrows, jays and robins but sparing the farm fowl. They learn quickly to be content only watching them, perhaps as intently as the cats watch Don Manuel de Zuniga's pet bird in Goya's painting, but with the same restraint. If anything, a cat is too trusting, as Cowper reminds one in a very funny poem about discovering one of his cats and her kittens complacently pawing and sniffing a large pit viper that had wound its way into his garden.

The long history of cats' companionship with people is eloquent testimony to their trust. Not even snakes have been more viciously abused than cats, and only snakes have been as frequently suspected of being in league with dark supernatural powers. They are more orderly than we are, much more attentive to personal cleanliness and generally more attentive to us than we are to one another.

Montaigne may have been right; cats may simply be amused at the conduct they elicit from us. No one is quite right in the head around a cat. The extravagant tales about people's devotion to cats that fill Oriental mythology must reflect at least some reality. The prophet Mohammed had a cat he loved dearly and for which he performed many unprophetic antics that are part of his history. Gautama Buddha was equally enchanted by his cat. The Egyptians who buried their mummified cats in Bubastis, along with mummified mice to keep them sated on their journey, would let their houses burn down—if we are to believe the historian Herodotus—while they scrambled through the flames to save the household cats. Here is James Boswell, writing about Samuel Johnson, in an age when London swells would hang cats, shoot them or drown them for sport: "I shall never forget the indulgence with which he treated Hodge his cat: for whom he himself used to go out and buy oysters, lest the servants having that

Van der Steen

trouble should take a dislike to the poor creature. I am, unluckily, one of those who have an antipathy to a cat, so that I am uneasy when in the room with one; and I own, I frequently suffered a good deal from the presence of this same Hodge. I recollect him one day scrambling up Dr. Johnson's breast, apparently with much satisfaction, while my friend smiling and half-whistling, rubbed down his back, and pulled him by the tail; and when I observed he was a fine cat, saying, 'Why yes, Sir, but I have had cats whom I liked better than this;' and then as if perceiving Hodge to be out of countenance, adding, 'but he is a very fine cat, a very fine cat indeed.'"

The oysters are a good reason for a cat putting up with someone. But cats have accompanied hobos and lonely travelers with little to offer but attention. Unlike most other animals, they have almost no occupations among us except as mousers. Yet they go everywhere with people, even—despite their reputation for disliking water—on ships; a merchant ship without its cat is scarcely a ship at all. Columbus and the first conquistadors brought cats with them to the New World, the first tame cats ever seen on these continents, and the Aztecs were immediately taken with them, calling them simply "little lions." In Southeast Asia cats were once said to be temple guards, although their duties, for instance in the temples of Thailand, seem to have been religious rather than constabulary; but Siamese cats are still trained as watch cats on barges in Bangkok. These are exceptions; on the

whole they seem attractive for their maddening independence and because they seem to enjoy being admired. Even the wise cleric who wrote the book of rules for nuns in the thirteenth century known as the *Ancrene Riwle*, while he cautioned them against becoming attached to anything earthly and forbade them to keep "any pet," made an allowance—"except a cat."

Well, cats are seductive. There is their grace and beauty, of course. But part of their charm is that they tend to be a little crazy. Their proverbial curiosity is part of it. The maniacal intensity of a cat's search into the unknown, or even into what it knows very well, is beyond reason, prediction or analysis. The cat seems to assume that either the whole creation is a trick or that nature and all other creatures are incompetent to get things done right. Shuffle papers in a file or move clothes or boxes in a closet and the cat will reexamine every scrap and thread, and make its own arrangements. The underside of a carpet, a hole anywhere, the space behind books on a shelf, cannot be left unexamined by this officious bureaucrat. And if it is denied entry it will soon learn to open doors and cabinets by swinging on the knobs.

Cats are the victims of their own senses; "nervous as a cat" is an accurate description. They cannot turn their ears completely off, or their noses for that matter. A recumbent cat, sound asleep, will suddenly shoot off in a flying leap at things no other animal senses, sometimes at nothing, and once it is on the move it is almost impossible to distract. Its leap is a wonderful expression, to

Van der Steen

be sure. It is amusing to watch crowds cheer athletes making high jumps under eight feet; to jump as high as a cat does in relation to its size one would have to rise up more than twenty feet from a standstill. Often cats appear to leap just for the fun of it, or without knowing why; they will bolt up into a tree or to the top of a cabinet and then betray some bewilderment about where they are. They do like being on top of things and seem nonplussed to be looked down at for long. Their pleasure in looking down at you from a limb or the top of a bookcase is manifest; it may come from their hunting instincts.

We understand so little about them, not even why they purr, for instance. We know as much about how the great stars form, operate and die as we do about a cat's purr. And even the cat does not seem to know why its tail is in such constant motion; often-times it seems surprised that the tail is moving at all. Young cats appear not to realize it is part of them until another cat, or they themselves, bite it, and even old cats will sometimes eye it suspiciously and try to pounce on it.

If cats tend to be on display most of the time, it is not just for us. Cats together, whether in great urban congregations like those in Rome, or merely a few assembled on a lawn, perform for one another constantly. And the competitive preening can be most impressive among a group of cats that have no one's attention to get but one another's. When they are together, they also betray a suspicion that their whole family is mad; a cat will react more

Van der Steen

quickly to the sudden movement of another cat than it will to one by a human being, faster than we would, or could, at the movement of a lion in tall grass.

Oh, but the cat is most admirable. We pay the great ones dreadful tribute, killing them so we can wear their skins, not as Hercules wore the lion's as a sign of strength, but in the ridiculous belief that in a great cat's skin we can look half as good as the cat. The small cats can be as astonishingly beautiful as any of the large forest or jungle cats. It is hard to believe they do not enjoy being looked at, and it takes a sense of proportion, and often a sense of humor, to avoid being completely taken in by them.

Van der Steen had a fine sense of humor about cats, and evidently about himself. His amusement is genuine. Just notice the care he takes, for instance, especially in the pen drawings, to catch the way a cat will turn its head to look at you; it is not strangeness in the attitude of the cats in the pictures that makes one smile, but precisely the familiarity of it. And he did not use cats to amuse us—the way Mozart or Ravel did when they wrote their songs for cats or even the way Cervantes did when he created Don Quixote's famous battle with the cats in his bedroom. He respected the nature of cat.

He was very delicate, for instance, in his choice of tree and bush as prop and background for his cats. Cats love plants and all green things. To see one sniffing and meditating leaf and branch, its eyes nearly closed, is to witness nirvana. It is not only the great valerian or the minty herb catnip cats delight in, but grass, leaf ginger, roses, the leaves of most berries, ivies and all kinds of trees, especially fruit trees. Van der Steen's cats are at home in trees— the painted ones certainly, but even some of those in the drawings. And odd trees they are. One appears to bear stars rather than leaves. Another has leaves or fruits, it is hard to know which, that resemble colored tumblers, window blind pulls, avocados or small gourds. All have varicolored leaves and one that bears recognizable fruit, though of the wrong color for its shape, has leaves like some sort of wilted bananas gone purple.

His point of view is a bit of trickery, of course; it is the view of a camera. His cats are humoring him, posing for him. They gaze into his camera oblivious of birds, butterflies or even their own kittens about them. Even the two that are coming down from branches toward a bird in the foreground are concentrating on the artist, not on the bird, which seems to be the only creature in the picture not quite sure of its standing. And if the cats in these pictures are losing bits of their feline identities, it is not to the artist or any other human, but to the world of plants. They are the stuff of artifice, but not artificial. They are pleased as punch, but cats usually are.

They are very odd, of course, but their oddity leads one to think more about cats than about the artist. In that way they are much closer to Goya's cats than, let us say, to Picasso's, which give one the feeling they are only there to demonstrate that the

Van der Steen

artist's style could transform anything and fit it into his singular world. Van der Steen offends virtuosity; his style mocks style but reveals his subject. His cats do not immediately make one think of the cats of other artists, literal, fantastic or otherwise. They conform to no one else's notions and yield little to any conventional representation or to the popular literature about cats. Their integrity springs from their establishment of a connection in the mind between real cats and their history and these pictures. Van der Steen looked at cats and was able to put into pictures not only what he saw but something that would invite the viewer of the pictures to look again at cats for himself.

Van der Steen

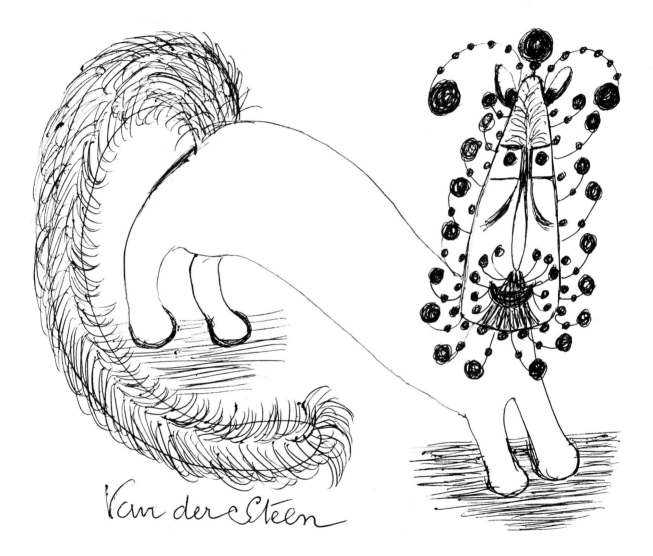

Van der Steen

Van der Steen

Van der Steen

Van der Sleez

Van der Steen

Van der Steen

Van der Steen

Van der Steen

Van der Steeg

Van der Steen

Van der Steen

ABOUT HIMSELF

MY mother brought me into this world on a hot July evening in 1897. It pleased the heavens to distinguish that night with a violent storm that inflicted great damage. Cataracts of rain plunged to the earth, and the sky, irradiated by strange bolts of lightning, caused a rumbling orchestral piece to resound, composed of ear-shattering harmonies and dissonances.

My childhood memories reach back to the years when the separation of church and state was being completed. I was the third child in a family that expanded regularly, year after year. My father, a deeply pious and upright man of honor, was a tireless worker and a businessman with many interests. He possessed a beautiful tenor, and on Sunday evenings we used to assemble in the parlor and listen full of enthusiasm as the paternal voice rendered the sonorous melody of "The Three Guarde Hussars."

My mother was an energetic and very cultivated woman. She had painted pictures, little masterpieces of charm and artistic deftness, which hung on the walls of our house and delighted my gaze. I think that I realized one of the dreams of her youth by becoming a painter.

We attended the Catholic school located on the Boulevard de la Reine in Versailles, where I learned the basics of drawing. When the season encouraged it, we rambled along the shady avenues of the Versailles palace park on schoolless Thursdays. In my young imagination the splendid pictures of the past arose anew. At every bend of the mysterious, quiet paths in the park, I expected to see the majestic procession of the Sun King appearing, with his courtiers and the prettiest ladies of the empire garbed in precious dresses shimmering with gold. From the somewhat more distantly situated copse of the queen, in contrast, the soft notes of ballets by Lully or spinets playing music by Rameau could be heard....

1910 was the year of the great flood in the Seine basin. Our parents decided to send us to the private school of the Frères de Passy, who had emigrated to Belgium. At this school in Froyennes near Tournai I began to draw and also become interested in watercolors.

1911–1912–1913—years of learning and of musing, cradled by the song of the wind that now and again whistles across the gigantic plains of the North in fierce storms, and by the music of the organ in the chapel, which was played by an artist (Brother Albert des Anges).

An uncanny memory. The tail of Halley's Comet came into sight in the atmosphere, causing a tumult. We beheld a great

milky gleam on the horizon. . . . From the wings of the world theater we already heard, muted, bellicose fanfares from beyond the Rhine!

July 1914. My parents sent me to England to perfect my knowledge of the language. My eyes feasted on the unique beauty of the English landscape. In six months I passed the examination at Oxford University with a grade of "good."

At the end of 1915 I am drafted into the French army. The ship passage across the channel is protected by steel nets from floating mines.

January 1916. Assigned to the 160th Infantry Regiment at Nevers. 1917, sent to the front at the Vosges. The cleric visiting our wounded is the future archbishop of Paris, Monsignor Feltin. In July 1918 some poison gas catches up with me during a clearing operation and I am evacuated. I was not to return to the front.

The armistice surprises me in Riom where I paint small watercolors of the area. I am demobilized in September 1919. Now my brother and I look for jobs in Paris although the city remains quite indifferent to the soldiers who are seeking to find their way back into civilian life. My father finally manages to have me assigned to a grade school in Lorraine, where I teach for three years. But the consequences of the gas poisoning force me to give up the job. Once again I am unemployed, until I find a government job, where I sometimes have enough freedom to make a few sketches.

1927–1928–1929–1930—gloomy, gray years of incessant exertion for my daily bread. Painting is my only diversion.

1931. My brother takes me along on his trips through various departments, which he visits for business reasons. We travel mostly through southern France, where I admire nature in its incomparable beauty and commit it to my memory. This work with my brother comes to an end on the unforgettable island of Corsica, with its magical climate and exceptional natural beauty. Again I must search out some other activity, living in the meantime from hand to mouth. I draw and paint small pictures, which I hang up in my room. Then I meet the woman who becomes my life's companion. Together we run a kind of drugstore. And here my calling as a painter truly breaks through. Between customers I paint watercolors and sell them to the people who stop to look at them.

The case of poisoning that I picked up in the war grows worse and worse. At night attacks of suffocation awaken me. And when I cannot sleep, I paint, paint unflaggingly.

In the oppressive silence of my long, sleepless nights, the harmonies within me transpose themselves into rhythms of color. Memories of beautiful concerts that I had attended earlier at the Théâtre des Champs Elysées, at the time of the great conductor René Battoz, return to my mind, and I express them in colorful visions. *The Accursed Huntsman*, by César Franck. *The Afternoon of a Faun*, by Claude Debussy, and so on. Creations crowd within

me, and above my head endless harmonies billow incessantly....

At that time I noticed that true creation of the spirit proceeds accompanied by pain, just as does physical birth. My works first saw the light of the world in a painful mental birth. In a fever of creativity, as if in divine intoxication, I succeeded in less than two years in painting thirty-two pictures that owe their creation to the great masters of music. *The Firebird*, by Stravinsky (reproduced in color in the album of *Figaro* in 1946). *Russian Easter* by Rimsky-Korsakov. *The Swan*, by Saint-Saëns. *The Spider's Feast*, by Albert Roussel, and so on. The critics have called me a visionary painter, and they are right. I remember that it took me three years to find the drawing and the colors that fitted the transposing of Saint-Saëns's *Danse Macabre*.

This period of painful, uninterrupted work burned me out and so exhausted me that I had to give up painting for a while. But later, too, when I took it up once more, I never again found the swift rhythm of that musical time. Looking back, I know now that I was living through a time of most intense experiencing, a period in which I felt myself truly possessed by the demon, or rather by the god of painting.

If there is a piece of music that precisely depicts those hallucinatory hours, then it is the fantastic ride of Mephistopheles and Faust in Berlioz's *Damnation of Faust*. Hopp! Hopp! cries Mephisto. An inner voice seemed to be crying to me, too: "Hopp! Hopp! Paint, don't stop painting, leap over the barriers, what do

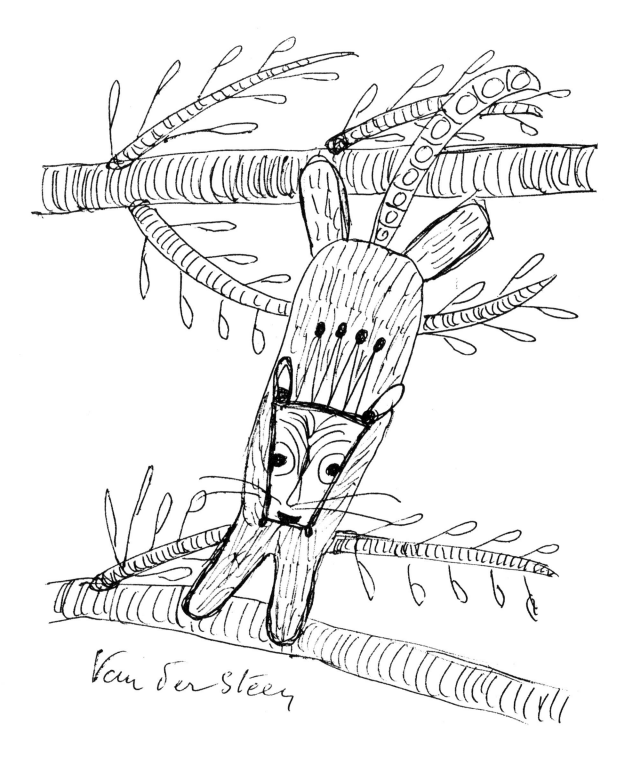

Van der Steen

you care about your health, what do you care about the time draining away! It is your destiny to paint, only and ever to paint...."

My most important public exhibitions were first the Salon d'Automne, 1944; the so-called Salon of Liberation, where I sold Madame Saint my first picture for eight thousand francs; then the Salon d'Automne in the following year, and finally in June 1946 a large exhibition of thirty pictures in the Galerie Clausen, for which the journalist and painter Henri Delanglade wrote an introduction. This exhibition, too, was a success. I was even asked to explain my music-inspired pictures in a radio interview. In 1946 I was invited to exhibit by the Salon des Tuileries. Then I sold ten pictures to Americans, and customers flowed into the store to see and buy my pictures.

In 1950 an exhibition of twenty-five fantasy pictures of animals and flowers took place in the Galerie Louise, for which Anatole Jakovsky wrote the introduction. As a result I received a visit from Mr. and Mrs. Hutter from Basel, who organized an exhibition of my music and fantasy pictures in their own gallery somewhat later on. This show produced echoes throughout all of Switzerland. A professor from the University of Basel bought several pictures. And I must not forget the encouragement and friendship that Dr. July and his wife afforded me; they, too, own numerous pictures and sketches of mine.

My last large exhibition took place in a gallery near the Place

de l'Etoile in October 1951; P. Mornand wrote the introduction. A large painting that I painted for my friend Camille Renault, the well-known restaurateur and art lover, was the reason for my break with that gallery, because they claimed exclusive rights to my pictures.

At the conclusion of this autobiography, I must report about a very strange attitude that has affected me vocationally as a painter: the hostility of my family. My wife and our two daughters, Gisèle and Nicole, have no regard whatsoever for my painting. Thus for a long time I had to put up with their daily mocking. For them my works are only doodlings and daubings. But considering the whole, my painting has brought me more solace and joy than unpleasantness, in spite of all such obtuseness. What do we care about storm and squall! The pilgrim trudges onward along his earthly path. And if I had to begin all over again, I would act no differently....

Frequently, then, I think of the wise proverb: "The dogs bark, the caravan passes by...." My work will outlive me.

Paris, April 26, 1954

ONE-MAN EXHIBITIONS:

Galerie Clausen, Paris.	1946
Introduction by Henri Delanglade	
Galerie Louise, Paris.	1950
Introduction by Anatole Jakovsky	
Galerie Hutter, Basel.	1950
Galerie Monique de Groote, Paris.	1951
Introduction by P. Mornand	
Galerie de la Radio, Paris.	1957
Introduction by Gisèle d'Assailly	
Galerie Maurice Raton, Paris.	1958
Galerie Toni Brechbuhl, Grenchen.	1963
Galerie Lutz and Meyer, Stuttgart.	1963
Introduction by A. Jakovsky	
Musée d'Art Primitif, Zagreb.	1964
Introduction by A. Jakovsky	
Galerie Michel Columb, Nantes.	1965
Introduction by A. Jakovsky	
Galerie Hilt, Basel.	1965